1950s

American scientists prove that pain is influenced by our thoughts and emotions. It is not purely physical.

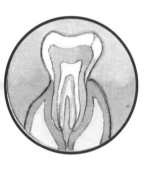

1840s

Anesthetics make childbirth, dentistry, and surgery pain-free for the first time.

1990s

U.S. scientists discover that men and women experience pain differently.

1880s

Neurons (nerve cells that carry electrical pain signals) are discovered.

2007

Brain scanners help doctors study the brain and investigate how it processes pain signals.

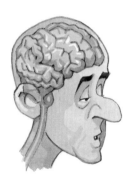

1980s

Chinese and American researchers show that long-lasting pain changes neurons in the brain, and makes us feel more pain.

Danger Pains – Don't Ignore!

Some pains can be the sign
of serious illness or injury,
for example:

- Severe pain after an accident or
  a fall
- Pain plus weakness or numbness
  in your arms or legs
- Pain in your chest, especially if
  it spreads to your arms or throat
- Bad headache with a stiff neck
  and/or skin rash and/or sensitivity
  to light
- Severe stomach pain

AS YOU READ, REMEMBER,
THIS BOOK IS NOT A DOCTOR!

The text and pictures in this book
are for interest and information
only. THEY ARE NOT MEDICAL
ADVICE. If you are worried about
pain of any kind, you should see
a doctor, nurse, or other health
professional.

Author:

Fiona Macdonald studied history at Cambridge University, England, and at the University of East Anglia. She has taught in schools, universities, and in adult education, and is the author of numerous books for children on historical topics.

Artist:

David Antram was born in Brighton, England, in 1958. He studied at Eastbourne College of Art and then worked in advertising for 15 years before becoming a full-time artist. He has illustrated many children's nonfiction books.

Series creator:

David Salariya was born in Dundee, Scotland. He has illustrated a wide range of books and has created and designed many new series for publishers in the UK and overseas. David established The Salariya Book Company in 1989. He lives in Brighton with his wife, illustrator Shirley Willis, and their son, Jonathan.

Editor: **Jacqueline Ford**

Editorial Assistant: **Mark Williams**

PAPER FROM
SUSTAINABLE
FORESTS

© The Salariya Book Company Ltd MMXVI
No part of this publication may be reproduced in whole or in part, or stored in a retrieval system, or transmitted in any form or by any means, electronic, mechanical, photocopying, recording, or otherwise, without written permission of the publisher. For information regarding permission, write to the copyright holder.

Published in Great Britain in 2016 by
The Salariya Book Company Ltd
25 Marlborough Place, Brighton BN1 1UB

ISBN-13: 978-0-531-21491-6 (lib. bdg.) 978-0-531-22441-0 (pbk.)

All rights reserved.
Published in 2016 in the United States
by Franklin Watts
An imprint of Scholastic Inc.

A CIP catalog record for this book is available
from the Library of Congress.

Printed and bound in China.
Printed on paper from sustainable sources.

1 2 3 4 5 6 7 8 9 10 R 25 24 23 22 21 20 19 18 17 16

You Wouldn't Want to Live Without™

Pain!

Written by
Fiona Macdonald

Illustrated by
David Antram

Series created by
David Salariya

Franklin Watts®
An Imprint of Scholastic Inc.

Contents

Introduction

Imagine living in a world without pain! You wouldn't get headaches, stomachaches, or toothaches. It wouldn't hurt when you touched something hot, or cut yourself, or fell down. A pain-free world may sound wonderful, but it would actually be disastrous. Why? Because pain has a purpose! What if you got a cut and didn't feel it? You might not clean it and it could get infected, making you sick without you knowing it. If pain did not exist, our lives would be very dangerous. We probably wouldn't survive for long. We would certainly be less healthy. And we'd probably feel less good about ourselves. For all these reasons, you really wouldn't want to live without pain. Read on, and find out more…

Life's a Pain

PROBLEMS DEEP INSIDE our bodies cause a dull and heavy pain that spreads over a wide area.

CRASH AND BANG. When we crush a limb or break a bone we feel a crashing, throbbing pain. It can be so intense that it makes you vomit.

SHORT, SHARP SHOCK. Touching a damaged nerve—for example in a tooth—creates a burning, stabbing pain, like an electric shock!

PAIN PUZZLE. We sometimes feel pain from one part of our body in another part of it. It's because pain signals sometimes get mixed up as they travel to our brain.

Pain is a part of life. Almost everyone suffers from it at one time or another. Pain may be mild and fleeting, or serious and long-lasting. It can be sharp and sudden or dull and grumbling. It aches, stings, stabs, throbs, grinds, or burns. It has many different causes: accidents, illnesses, injuries, twists, turns, falls, fights, and bites. However, most pain is the result of ordinary, everyday activities. All around the world, millions of people suffer pain that, with care, could be avoided. What a shame!

Sit up! Don't slump!

Ponytails pull painfully.

Badly fitting shoes? Agony!

Eyestrain? Get new glasses!

You'll get a backache if you bend incorrectly.

Junk food may give you indigestion!

Don't be a weekend warrior! That's what doctors call someone who doesn't exercise on weekdays, but takes part in extreme sports on weekends. "Weekend warriors" often end up with broken bones and strained muscles—and a lot of pain.

Marathon

Tender thumbs?
Too much texting!

SMALL PAINS, BIG PROBLEMS. Some everyday aches and pains may seem a bit silly, but they are no laughing matter!

- In 2009, almost half of American adults said that pain interfered with their work and their enjoyment of life.

- In 2009, 42 million Americans claimed that their sleep was interrupted by pain.

- In 2013, 31 million working days were lost in the UK because of everyday pain. Pain in the back, neck, and muscles was the most common reason why workers stayed home.

- In 2013, British workers took twice as many days off for sickness as workers in the United States.

Fat wallet,
tight pants:
surprisingly sore.

Be careful
carrying
heavy loads!

Pace yourself;
avoid sports
injuries.

Stress makes our
muscles feel stiff
and sore.

Painful Past

For people who lived long ago, life would probably have been full of pain. There were few or no doctors, nurses, hospitals, or safe, inexpensive painkilling medicines to help them. They might even have believed that the pain was all their fault. The word *pain* came from Ancient Rome and originally meant "punishment," sent by fate, nature, or the gods. Today, thousands of years later, we have different ideas about pain. Doctors and scientists have discovered that pain happens when a human body is damaged or disturbed. It is not sent by an outside power.

PAYBACK TIME. The ancient Hindus believed in Karma: Good actions will be rewarded, and bad ones punished. Today we have a similar saying: "What goes around comes around."

ALL IN THE MIND. Greek philosopher Plato did not think that pain was punishment. Instead, he described it as a "passion of the soul" felt in the mind, not the body.

It's punishment! You deserve your pain!

For centuries, in many lands, pain was used to torture prisoners and punish criminals. But in 1791, the Eighth Amendment to the U.S. Constitution banned "cruel and unusual punishments" —and set a good example to governments worldwide.

THE GREAT DOCTOR. Muslim scholar Ibn Sina (980–1037) was one of the first to understand that we feel pain because our bodies suffer injury or illness.

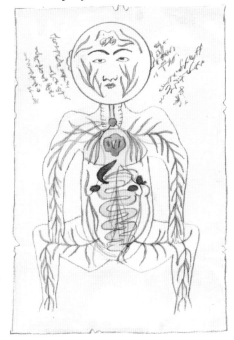

PAIN MACHINE. In a work published in 1664, French scientist René Descartes suggested that pain is a process: a series of movements that transmit sensations through the body. He described his theory in a word-picture. "Imagine a hand holding a rope leading to the brain. When a hammer hits the hand, painful pressure on the hand shakes the rope. The shaking travels along the rope and rings a bell in the brain."

Pain Pathways

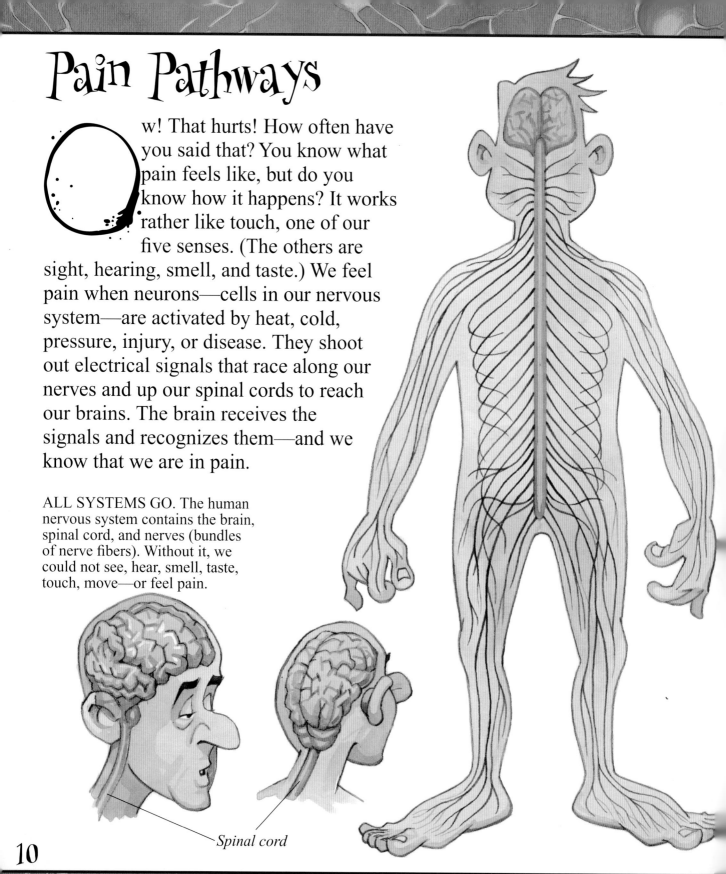

Ow! That hurts! How often have you said that? You know what pain feels like, but do you know how it happens? It works rather like touch, one of our five senses. (The others are sight, hearing, smell, and taste.) We feel pain when neurons—cells in our nervous system—are activated by heat, cold, pressure, injury, or disease. They shoot out electrical signals that race along our nerves and up our spinal cords to reach our brains. The brain receives the signals and recognizes them—and we know that we are in pain.

ALL SYSTEMS GO. The human nervous system contains the brain, spinal cord, and nerves (bundles of nerve fibers). Without it, we could not see, hear, smell, taste, touch, move—or feel pain.

Spinal cord

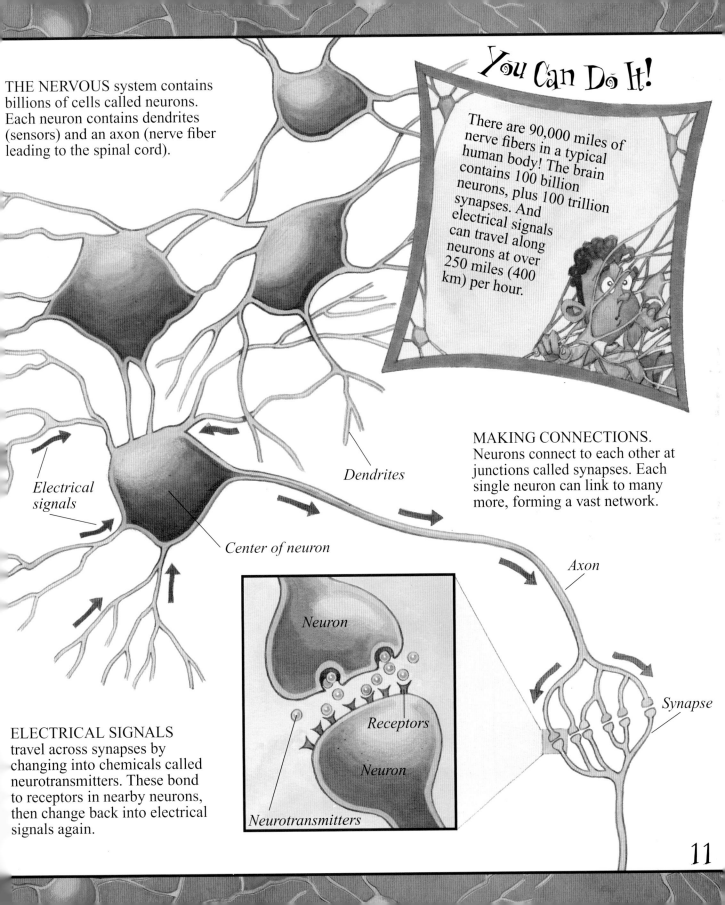

THE NERVOUS system contains billions of cells called neurons. Each neuron contains dendrites (sensors) and an axon (nerve fiber leading to the spinal cord).

You Can Do It!

There are 90,000 miles of nerve fibers in a typical human body! The brain contains 100 billion neurons, plus 100 trillion synapses. And electrical signals can travel along neurons at over 250 miles (400 km) per hour.

Electrical signals

Center of neuron

Dendrites

MAKING CONNECTIONS. Neurons connect to each other at junctions called synapses. Each single neuron can link to many more, forming a vast network.

Axon

Synapse

Neuron

Receptors

Neuron

Neurotransmitters

ELECTRICAL SIGNALS travel across synapses by changing into chemicals called neurotransmitters. These bond to receptors in nearby neurons, then change back into electrical signals again.

11

Touchy-Feely

So neurons carry pain signals. But how do we sense the difference between a gentle caress and a painful punch? By different types of neurons. Some neurons send signals only when they detect light pressure. That means we feel pleasure. Others react only to sharp, sudden sensations. That means we feel pain. Now—here's another puzzle. Have you ever wondered why a tiny cut on your finger can hurt so much? It's because dendrites (nerve endings) are not spread evenly through our bodies. Most are in our lips—and our fingertips!

WEAK WOMEN? Strong men? Not so! Studies show that men and women experience pain differently. On average, women suffer more pain than men do. They are better able to express their emotions about being in pain, and they cope better with extreme pain than men do.

Different Nerve Fibers

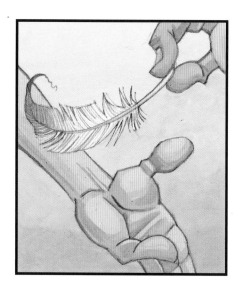

TENDER TOUCH. A-beta nerve fibers are easily activated. They carry electrical signals from gentle sensations, like light tickles.

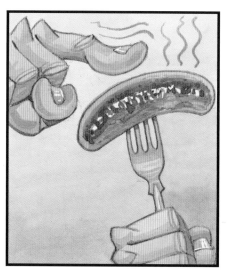

HOT STUFF! A-delta fibers sense heat and sudden strong movements. They carry signals from painful sensations, like intense heat.

STEADY GOING. C-fibers carry signals from harmful chemicals, heat, and pressure, but they work slowly. That's why some pain, like from a bruise, lasts a long time.

PAIN MAN. This strange-looking model shows how nerve endings are concentrated in the body. The model's biggest body parts have the most nerve endings and feel the strongest pain. The smallest body parts have the fewest nerve endings and are the least sensitive.

How It Works

Doctors describe sudden, short-lived pain as acute (brief and sharp). They call pain that continues for weeks or months chronic (long-lasting). Both are bad—it's hard to say which makes us more miserable.

AAARGH! That feels like a million nerve endings!

Mind, Body, Spirit...

We all have similar nervous systems, but each of us feels pain a little differently. My pain is not the same as yours, or his, or hers. Why is this? Partly, it's the way our bodies are made. Some people are more sensitive to pain, others less so. But mostly it's because we sense pain in our minds as well as our bodies. When our brains receive electrical signals from neurons, they mix them with our ideas, beliefs, memories, hopes, and fears, to create our own personal pain experience.

Mind Over Matter

LOVELY LADIES long ago wore tight, painful corsets to make their waists look slimmer. They said "We must suffer to be beautiful."

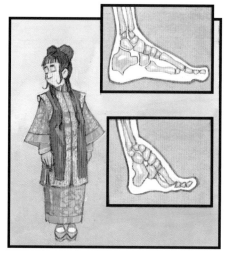

FOOT FASHIONS. Chinese mothers used to twist and bind their daughters' bones to create tiny "lily feet." This painful custom was banned in 1912.

FANCY FACES. Many people put up with considerable pain to decor their skin. For the Maori people of New Zealand, facial tattoos were traditionally a sign of rank and pov

Brokenhearted? Yes, it's true! Love, hate, and other feelings can cause physical pain. We say we are "sick with worry," or "grief has broken my heart." When we feel strong emotions like these, our brain sends electrical signals to the rest of our body, causing painful sensations.

FEEL THE FEAR. Whatever we believe, pain teaches us to be careful, and to keep an eye out for danger. And the fear of a fierce and painful attack makes us run away—very quickly!

HOLY HERMITS gave up worldly comforts to try to feel closer to Heaven. They willingly endured cold, hunger, and pain.

STIFF UPPER LIP. Traditionally, British men did not like to show their feelings in public. They believed it was better to suffer in silence.

UNBEARABLE! Medieval Christians used to wear scratchy, itchy hair shirts as a punishment, to show that they were sorry for their sins.

15

Brainless = Painless?

You're a human! You can think and reason, learn from your experiences, and express ideas and feelings in words. You can do all this because you have a wonderful brain and sensitive, fast-acting nerves. But what about other living creatures with smaller, simpler, less developed nervous systems? Do they experience pain? If so, how does this happen? Does being injured hurt them? Do they suffer? Do they care? At the moment, scientists don't have enough information to know for sure. But they are working hard to find the answers.

LIKE HUMANS, fish have nerves that can carry pain signals. Some scientists think fish brains can't recognize these signals, and so fish don't feel pain. Others disagree.

NOT OLD ENOUGH? Until the 20th century, doctors believed that babies could not feel pain, because their nervous systems were not fully developed.

NOTHING TO SAY? Because animals can't use words to describe bad sensations, people used to think that they didn't suffer pain.

CRABS AND some other invertebrates (creatures without backbones) also have nerves that can detect painful sensations.

Why has nature made it that most insects don't feel pain? Probably because they don't live long enough for pain to be useful. For example, mayflies don't have time to learn from painful experiences. Once they become winged adults, they live for only about 24 hours.

CHECK THIS OUT.

To find out if a creature can feel pain, scientists search for these signs:

- It has a nervous system with pain sensors
- It seems aware of its surroundings
- It produces electrical signals in the brain when injured
- It changes behavior (e.g. limps, runs away) when injured
- Painkilling chemicals affect its brain
- It can learn to avoid painful danger

FLOWERS, TREES, and fungi don't have nerves or brains. As far as we know, they have no way of sensing pain.

17

What's the Point of Pain?

Now that we know *how* we sense pain, we need to ask *why* we feel it. The answer is simple: Pain keeps us safe. It warns and protects us, and other living creatures as well. The world is full of dangers—blazing fires, sharp stones, and more. Pain teaches us to avoid them: Look Out! Stay Away! Be Careful! Without pain, we would soon get injured or maybe even kill ourselves by accident. Many plants and animals would also not survive if they didn't have ways of causing pain to others. A world without pain would be a nightmare!

PROTECTED BY PAIN. Plants guard themselves against harmful pests by growing sharp thorns and prickles.

A LOT TO LEARN. Early people and their pets were surrounded by painful dangers. But if they learned from their pain they were more likely to survive.

TOXIC TREE. Australia's Gympie-Gympie tree contains powerful chemicals in hairs on its leaves. These irritate nerve endings in the skin of people who touch them, producing itching, swelling, and pain.

SMALL BUT DEADLY. Tiny, fragile creatures such as bees, wasps, and scorpions use pain to protect themselves against larger, stronger enemies. The venom they inject always hurts, and sometimes kills!

Top Tip

Heed these painful warnings: Sunburn warns us that our skin is being damaged by the Sun's rays. Frostbite tells us that our flesh is being destroyed by freezing cold. Avoid both if you can!

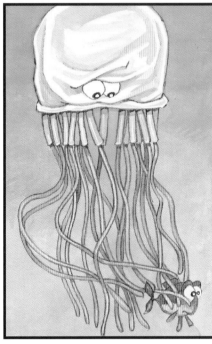

SUPER STINGER. The lion's mane jellyfish is soft and floppy. It can't fight or run away. But its stingers cause agonizing, paralyzing pain, and make it one of the sea's most fearsome creatures.

Safety, Sympathy, Survival

Why do we go to bed when we feel tired or sick? Because pain is protecting and teaching us! It makes us want to lie down in a quiet, safe place, and we soon learn that this helps us to recover more quickly. Pain also teaches us to treat our bodies—and other people—with respect. If we do bad or stupid things to harm ourselves or others, we can expect to suffer in return. But if we are kind and sensible, then we and our friends, families, and communities all have a better chance of living a peaceful, pain-free existence.

MAGIC CURES MISERY? In the past, healers mixed magical, mysterious remedies. These could not cure disease, but gave hope and comfort to patients and made pain easier to bear.

HERO HELPERS. Soldiers risk death and danger to rescue their injured comrades. They hope that their friends will do the same for them one day, if necessary.

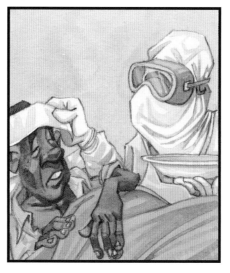

MERCY MISSION. Caring for others makes the world a less painful place. One example is the brave nurses trying to stop the spread of the deadly Ebola virus.

MY TURN! Parents and grandparents care for children until they can survive on their own. In return, children often help them when they grow old.

Trained first-aid workers soothe pain and save lives. If you are old enough, why not find out how you can help them? You could also ask your school to teach you and your friends some simple first-aid skills.

No Pain, No Gain

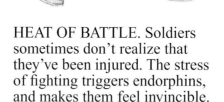

Great GOAAAALL!

How do you feel after playing football? Or dancing for hours? You're probably exhausted—but also happy and excited. When we push our bodies to achieve their very best, our nervous systems help us by producing special "feel-good" chemicals called endorphins. These natural painkillers block the normal electrical signals that are sent to the brain. So instead of feeling pain, we feel superhuman!

HEAT OF BATTLE. Soldiers sometimes don't realize that they've been injured. The stress of fighting triggers endorphins, and makes them feel invincible.

EXTRA ENERGY. Exercise improves our mood, as well as our fitness. The endorphins produced when we work out make us feel happy, positive, and energetic.

The Next Day

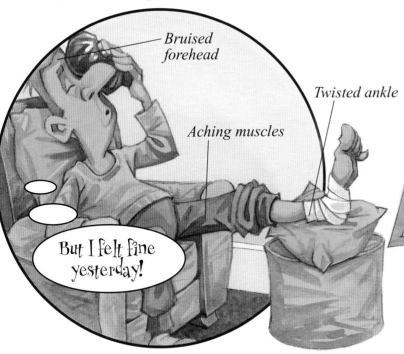

Bruised forehead

Aching muscles

Twisted ankle

But I felt fine yesterday!

You Can Do It!

Some of us love energetic team sports, others prefer gentle exercise, alone. It doesn't matter which you choose, as long as you keep active. Any regular, gentle exercise is good for you.

EASY DOES IT! Exercise keeps us strong and healthy, but don't overdo it! Top athletes are careful not to exercise too much, to make sure they don't damage their bodies while endorphins are still blocking pain.

GRACE AND PAIN. While she's on stage, a dancer puts all her energy into giving a great performance. Endorphins mean that she doesn't notice how much her feet hurt.

ONWARD AND UPWARD! Mountaineers find that the thrill of climbing produces natural painkillers. These give them the strength and energy to continue their adventures.

23

Painkillers?

f you had lived long ago, you would have expected to suffer pain. And, although your religion may have viewed pain as a punishment, you would have wished for something—anything—to take the pain away. But what to choose? Painkilling medicines were sometimes poisonous: They killed patients, as well as pain. Loud music forced you to forget your agony, but only for a short while. However, two ancient treatments did seem to work: acupuncture and gentle touch, although nobody at the time understood why. Today, doctors think that both stopped electrical pain signals carried by neurons reaching the brain.

WIPED OUT? Muslim doctors told patients to breathe vapor from a soporific (sleep-inducing) sponge soaked in painkilling medicines. Unfortunately, some never woke up!

UNBALANCED? The ancient Chinese technique of acupuncture —still used today—aimed to cure pain by improving energy flow in the body. Needles were stuck into patients at special places in the body. See figure at right.

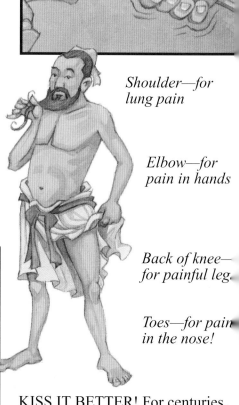

Shoulder—for lung pain

Elbow—for pain in hands

Back of knee—for painful leg.

Toes—for pain in the nose!

KISS IT BETTER! For centuries, mothers have known that a gentle kiss and a hug can soothe pain. The comforting touch relaxes us, blocks pain signals, and lowers levels of brain chemicals that make us extra-sensitive to pain.

FEEL THE BEAT.
Early dentists employed drummers to play very loudly when they pulled out rotten teeth. The noisy music was meant to overpower patients' senses and take their minds off their suffering. It hid screams of pain as well.

How It Works

Studies have shown that fake medicines can help to ease some patients' pain. But they only work if the patient believes they are real, and trusts the person who provides the medicine.

What a Relief

Hooray for Queen Victoria! In 1853, she demanded (and received) the latest scientific pain relief. Millions of people copied her, and a whole new era of "painless" medicine began. Since around 1500, pioneer doctors and scientists had already been trying to find better ways of easing pain. They experimented with microscopes and chemicals, and they traveled the world in search of painkilling plants. They finally had a breakthrough around 1840, and managed to develop anesthetic drugs that made patients unconscious and completely unable to feel pain.

ENOUGH'S ENOUGH!
Queen Victoria went through childbirth seven times without painkillers, but sniffed chloroform, an anesthetic vapor, for the births of her last two children. She described its effects as "soothing, quieting, and delightful."

Advances in Anesthetics

800–1200 CE
Patients sniff soporific (sleep-inducing) sponges, full of dangerous painkillers.

600 BCE
Doctors in India make patients drowsy with smoke from burning herbs.

How It Works

In 1779, German doctor Franz Mesmer found an unusual way of easing pain: hypnosis. Mesmer's patients fell into a trance. They could not feel pain. And when they woke up, they couldn't remember anything that had happened.

1770s–1840s
Top British scientists experiment with anesthetics.

1847
James Simpson discovers the anesthetic use of chloroform.

1840s
Doctors in the U.S. are the first to do surgical operations using gas anesthetics.

A HAPPY ACCIDENT?
Scottish doctor James Simpson was determined to find a new anesthetic, to ease pain in childbirth, dentistry, and surgical operations. So he experimented on himself and his friends. In 1847, one evening, they sniffed a liquid called chloroform. They quickly became unconscious—and woke up the next morning. Simpson was delighted; here was his new painkiller. It became very popular, although it sometimes killed patients. Modern anesthetics are much safer!

The Painful Truth

Today, in countries with modern medical services, we don't expect our lives to be full of pain. Science has shown us how and why pain happens, and doctors can usually control it with medications, anesthetics, and medical machines. Compared with people in the past, and with citizens of developing nations, we are extremely fortunate. Even so, we are never completely free of pain—and that's a good thing! A painless life would be difficult, dangerous, and probably deadly. Believe it or not, you really wouldn't want to live without pain!

HOUSEHOLD DANGERS:
1. Hot water
2. Swinging doors
3. Sharp knives
4. Hot stoves
5. Broken glass
6. Falls
7. Ball games
8. Low ceilings
9. Toys to trip over
10. Sharp knitting needles
11. Cat scratches
12. Fire
13. Bike accidents

IF YOU COULDN'T feel pain, home sweet home would be a death trap! When out and about, you'd cut and bruise yourself or break your bones without noticing. You'd get sick and not seek treatment—and your teeth might rot away. Travel, shopping, gardening, and sports would all be risky—and so would eating a meal with a knife and fork!

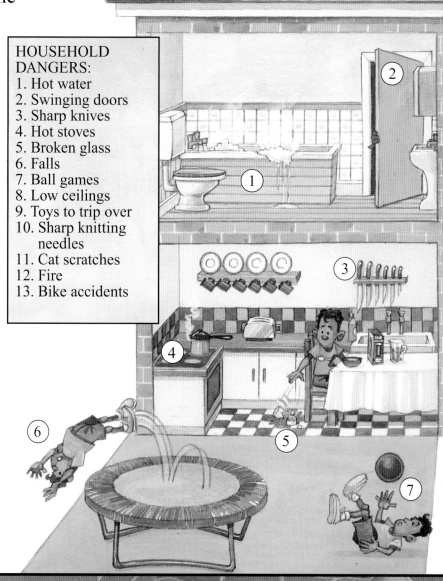

How It Works

Spinal cord

What happens when we touch something hot? When we sense pain, electrical signals activate motor neurons in our spinal cord. These send urgent signals back to our muscles, telling them to move our hand away. Because our brain is not involved, we do this automatically, without thinking.

8

9

10

12

11

13

AMERICAN Ashlyn Blocker cannot feel pain. Her life has been full of unexpected dangers, but scientists hope that studying her rare genetic condition will help them find new treatments for incurable pain.

Glossary

Acupuncture Traditional Chinese method of healing and pain relief, using needles. It is said to balance the flow of Chi (energy) through the body.

Acute Sharp.

Anesthetics Drugs that make patients unconscious for a short while, so that they do not feel pain.

Axon A long, threadlike part of a neuron (nerve cell). Also called a nerve fiber.

Chronic Long-lasting.

Dendrite Tiny sensor that stretches out from the center of a neuron.

Endorphins Natural painkilling chemicals produced by the body during exercise or other vigorous activity.

Fungi A large "family" of living things that includes mushrooms, toadstools, yeast, and molds.

Genetic condition A disease or disability caused by missing or faulty genes.

Hair shirt Tunic made of rough, itchy animal hair or plant fibers, worn next to the skin.

Humors Ancient Greek doctors thought that human bodies contained four humors: blood, water, yellow bile, and black bile. Too much or too little of these made people ill.

Hypnosis A technique used by healers to make patients fall into a trance (dreamlike state) where they are not aware of their surroundings and cannot feel pain.

Invertebrates Creatures that do not have a backbone, such as crabs.

Invincible Cannot be defeated.

Karma A traditional belief among Hindus in India that good actions will bring rewards and bad actions will bring punishment or misfortune.

Motor neurons Neurons that carry electrical signals controlling movements of the human body.

Nerves Fibers that carry electric signals to and from the brain. Each nerve is a bundle of smaller fibers, or axons.

Nervous system The body system made up of the brain, spinal cord, and nerves.

Neurons Cells in nerves, the spinal cord, and the brain. They receive and pass on electrical signals. There are different types of neurons, carrying separate signals about pain, movement, touch, and so on.

Neurotransmitters Chemicals that pass electrical signals from one neuron to another.

Receptor Area on the surface of a cell that can receive electrical signals from outside the cell.

Soporific Sleep inducing.

Spinal cord A thick bundle of nerves that runs inside the human backbone. It links the brain to nerves in the rest of the body.

Synapse Place where neurons connect to each other.

Toxic Poisonous, polluting.

Unconscious Not aware of who we are or our surroundings.

Venom Poison injected by bites or stings.

Index

Tell Me How It Hurts...

If you were a doctor, what would you do if a patient said, "Help! It feels like there's an elephant sitting on my chest!"? You'd probably act quickly, because chest pains can be the sign of serious illness. But it's not always easy to describe pain—or to understand somebody else's description of it.

We can feel pain, but we can't see it, smell it, or take a picture of it. And it's difficult to measure, because we can't tell whether our pain's the same as pain felt by others. So how do we try to understand someone else's pain? Here are a few ways:

Ask the patient to give his or her pain a score from 1 to 10, with 1 meaning the pain is very mild and 10 meaning it is unbearable.

Ask the patient to compare the pain to something completely different:

"It's like a metal band tight around my head."

"It's like a wave sweeping through my body."

- Ask the patient to find the best words to describe the pain.

There are 30 pain words listed below. Can you add any more?

Acute, Agonizing, Angry, Bad, Boring, Burning, Chronic, Cramping, Dull, Extreme, Gnawing, Grinding, Grumbling, Harsh, Heavy, Lacerating, Pinching, Prickling, Pulsing, Raging, Raw, Scalding, Sharp, Shooting, Stabbing, Stinging, Tingling, Throbbing, Violent, Vicious…

Using all of this information, people often find it easier to describe how they feel to someone else and get help for their pain.

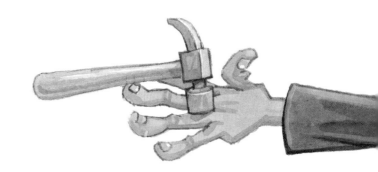

Top Tips to Ease Pain

Not too interested in sipping a mixture of poisonous herbs as a painkiller? Then try some of these nonmedical techniques to ease pain.

- Massage is one of the world's oldest pain-relieving techniques. It helps to relax muscles, improves blood flow, and may stop electrical pain signals getting to the brain.

- Relaxation methods help to make patients less tense and better able to cope with pain. Relaxation can help patients sleep, give them more energy, and reduce their anxiety.

- Dare to daydream! Use your imagination to escape from pain for a while. Picture a lovely place, friends and family, your favorite things. It's a great feeling!

- Ignore that pain! Read a great book, play music, enjoy a hobby, or go for a walk. All can help take people's minds off pain.

- Press pain away. Acupressure and Reiki use careful pressure on certain places in the body. Like acupuncture, they aim to balance energy, and may block pain signals.

- Bend and stretch. Gentle exercise, such as Tai Chi (an ancient Chinese martial art) and Yoga (from India) encourage calm, improve balance, and increase strength.

- Tune in! Biofeedback machines teach patients to control their heart rate, breathing, and blood pressure. This helps them to manage stress and reduce pain.